"Lyric, imagistic, and visionary, full of life and ever conscious of death, the poems in Miriam Sagan's *What Solitude Sees in Me: Uncollected Poems 1976–2023* roam inner and outer worlds with, as often as not, a motel room for home base. An uneclipsed poet of eclipses and the moon in general; the turn of seasons, winter in particular; geological as well as diurnal time; and all varieties of the metaphysical, Sagan writes with a deliberately homespun, often short line that lures us out to reel us in. The poems in this career-spanning volume leap the cosmos and stick their landing. I am grateful to have them under one roof."

— Carol Moldaw, author of *Go Figure*

"*What Solitude Sees in Me: Uncollected Poems 1976–2023* is a selected volume of Miriam Sagan's personal and (mostly) unpublished archives that are just now seeing the light of day. A generous and illuminating tour of words to be sure, these rich and varied poems are a journey into her past, her language topographies, from Manhattan to Chaco Canyon and, predominantly, New Mexico. From the intimate ('the body burns into its own echo') to the expansive ('You are so deep into America you cannot get out'), these aren't previously rejected or neglected works so much as reconsiderations of the poet's lifelong spirited and lyrical terrains. They include family, curiosity (of course), and solitude. What solitude sees in her, the rest of us see as well. Many of her passions and formative experiences are explored in this beautiful and revelatory collection."

— John Macker, author of *Desert Threnody* and *Belated Mornings*

What Solitude Sees in Me

Selected works by Miriam Sagan

Poems:
Archaeology of Desire
Border Line
Star Gazing
Seven Places in America

Nonfiction:
A Hundred Cups of Coffee
Searching for a Mustard Seed
Bluebeard's Castle

Fiction:
Commune of the Golden Sun
Black Rainbow
Shadow on the Minotaur

Miriam
Sagan
**What Solitude
Sees in Me**

Uncollected
Poems
1976-2023

Casa Urraca Press
A B I Q U I Ú

Author photograph by Matt Morrow.
Cover photograph by Zach Hively.
Set in Cardo and Glacial Indifference.

28 27 26 25   1 2 3 4 5 6 7

First edition

ISBN 978-1-956375-36-7

CASA URRACA PRESS

an imprint of Casa Urraca, Ltd.
PO Box 1119
Abiquiú, New Mexico 87510
casaurracapress.com

To Isabel.

Contents

I'm certainly not the only writer who at the age of seventy has a file cabinet full of mysterious manila folders. They might be obscurely labeled "drafts" or "poems" or even "Income tax—1986." And they might contain almost anything. That last one housed a copy of my second book, *True Body*, in manuscript form. Add to this the electronic equivalent on a computer desktop, which contains frighteningly named folders including "Death" and "Miscellaneous," and it is no surprise that I never open any of these.

However, aging, some anxious death cleaning, and the need to send everything to the Wittliff Collections at the library at Texas State, San Marcos, where my work is archived, led me to nervously start looking at things. And what did I find? Poems. A lot of them. Many that were published in books, some obvious failures, and some that seemed to have been written by me (or someone of the same name) but that lacked vitality. OK, fine, off to the archive or the garbage can.

But I was also finding poems that I liked, and that were meaningful to me, that had never appeared in any book. And why was that? My first husband, Robert Winson (1959–1995), was a small press editor and a great reader. He used to criticize my manuscripts by saying that I always left out quirky or off-brand work. "You just include capital-P Poems," he'd complain. Of course I ignored this feedback.

Until now. I started pulling those poems I liked and stacking them. I then created three stacks: *yes, no,* and *maybe*. As is often the case, *maybe* was pretty much *no*.

I added a few things. I took more out. When I looked at it, it seemed I had a book of poetry.

And what was it about? New Mexico, of course, where I've lived since 1984. And the greater Southwest region, from Las Vegas, Nevada, to the Mexico-Arizona border. And history, biology, geology, religion, botany—all the pursuits I love. But what struck me most was that, among some love poems and poems of motherhood and friendship, the theme that predominated was solitude. There I was, alone in a hotel in Mountainair, New Mexico, as if it were a monk's cell. Eating out alone in Salida, Colorado. By myself in salt flats, roadside motels, and in my own imagination. The oldest poem in this collection is "Fever Tropics," where I was alone with a serious illness when I was twenty-one. The poem isn't about the hospital, but rather an interior terrain.

Inner and outer worlds can never be reconciled by a poet, nor should they be. However, traveling between these two, and trying to express the experience in words, is something I'm grateful to have spent my life doing.

※

Acequia

Water runs cold in the ditch.
All the luck, and all the money
can't get you what you think you want
in this dry country.

※

The End of Ur

All things have their source: river, love, destruction.
It's narrow, birth canal, arroyo.
The conquerors
will marry in, die of the local
river parasites
imprint their grasslands, DNA, and gods.

One brick to ziggurat
ten thousand years
agriculture equals temple whore, Manhattan.
Abraham left Ur,
silver ram
caught in a golden thicket.
X-rays show torsos marked
by bacteria as old as mud
spirochete, sclerosis
Hagar in the wilderness
Raven says...

Glass case smashed
Assyrian gate smashed
even the skeleton looted of its rings.
This literally was the disappearance
of history...
into another narrative?
or simply an end?

Shanidar cave of Neanderthals,
graves sprinkled with wildflowers
(like us)
hand with arthritis
grape hyacinth, hollyhock.

Irrigation in this hot dry land
which will eventually
salinize the soil.
When belief becomes architecture
the spade turns up
one more silver coin with the moon in profile,
coin with a waning king.
Maybe we should never
have plowed this earth
in the first place.

※

Not Watching the Eclipse

A pinprick in paper—
image of the sun
made crescent by darkness
made moon by day.

A green light over water
and in the shadow of leaves
millions of eclipses
playing in interstices.

Camera obscura
unlit at noon
the luminous heart
and eyelid of bone.

※

Fever Tropics

There, among pale lianas,
coral-colored vines, and
fuchsias, where
the golden coils of cobras
mark leaf and shadow
with bright striations,
mapmakers label the latitude
fever.

Far below that green equator
heat unpeels my tissued skin,
my mouth parched for oxygen.
Tropic of Capricorn, Tropic of Cancer
erase all memory of snow.
Seduced to slow dissolve, I must let go.
The body burns into its own echo.

※

Found in a Library Book

Black and white snapshots:
smiling soldier leaves for Nam,
two couples the night of St. Mike's prom,
a fiftieth wedding anniversary…
anonymous, strangely emotional
they drop out at the turn
of a page in an unrelated narrative
as if something borrowed
must be returned.

※

Tent Rocks

Night has folded its wings
packed up its tents
towards morning.

We walk infolded in the slot
    canyon
    feminine space.

Your ten-year-old self says:
this is my bedroom, this my parlor
in the vast exposed roots of the ponderosa,

    soft eddy of sand
    striations of what fell
    from the sky.

Earth came from above
volcanic spew
pumice and ash—pyroclastic fragments

(the Greek for both
"fire" and "broken").
Hoodoos of stone like so many gremlins,

shapes in the mind.
What the trail marker says:
Stop—look here

as if there were no need to look
    to the right
    to the left

    red flower
    against geologic time
    a snatch of conversation.

In rock a potter's wheel
rising the height of a house
like a Claes Oldenburg clothespin

or some other
common household object
enlarged to heroic scale

colossus, a triumphal arch
a conquering general
on a gigantic horse.

What you see
    bigger
    smaller

than us
the meteor blazing
as it approaches earth

lands the size
of a grain of sand
in your burnt hand.

Time has folded the tents of day
until the long-haired
evening star

rises in the smoking mirror
and in the underwater world
of the lake below.

Eat an apple
bury its core
try to see

before language
separated me
from this world

before I knew
the name of the yellow gossamer
butterfly floating through this canyon's

Eden of rock.

※

Avoidance of the Blue

Like suffering, this forest can only be entered.
Snowfall lit at intervals by incarnadine lanterns.

That lost blue of dusk: medieval, cobalt, peacock.
Will the flute go on playing in the empty room?

※

Blue numbers
tattooed
on the old woman's arm
ahead in line
of my brother
at the all-night
delicatessen
in Brooklyn.
It was snowing
he was carrying
a paper cup of coffee
two pastries in a white bag.
He wanted
to say something
to her
but he
didn't know what
to say.

※

Darkness Darkness

I dreamed I dined on stew
of innards in a white bowl
liver and kidney
I ate my guts out.
First thing in the morning
on the unmade bed
I pull The Moon from the Tarot deck
"A good time for dreaming," she says.
The wheel rolls round to winter
the streets are full of rain
men fill vacant lots
with the carcasses of evergreens.
The solstice child
is turning in the womb
light is impatient
waiting to be born
again.
Moon says: I know all that.
Want to understand light and darkness?
Follow me
for I grow thin only
to grow fat.

※

the brass Tara
covered in pine needles
winter deepens

※

Ellis Island—
my daughter stands
in a green styrofoam crown
one hand held up
on the ferry, like a minuscule
Statue of Liberty, smiling,
lady without feet
in New York Harbor.
Still in the rear hall
chatter of living tourist and dead traveler,
faces of Yugoslavia, Greece, Poland, Trinidad.
The past was never so clear.
My daughter weeps
as if this were still a point
of embarkation
"I want to go home
to Santa Fe, my favorite
place on earth," she sobs.

I take her down
iron steps
surrounded by an iron cage
white hexagonal tiles.
Even I'm afraid
of something in this hall.
Island recedes
we face
again a blue Manhattan
staring like Narcissus
at its own reflection in the water.
The past is behind us
diminishing as indeed
we think it should.

※

Drawing white objects—
bowl, cup, sake jar.
The snow
is a kind of girl
wistful
in her art student league bun,
psalm of white unmarked paper

A winter's sun
after All Soul's Day
with its rice and beans.
Marigold petals freeze,
in the election booth
we vote on water
evil or less evil men.

You stay up reading
half the night. The phrase
"rivers of water"
means something to a child
born on Manhattan's west side
where the moon
climbs into a tugboat Hudson.

※

White Psalm

1.

Snow is writing with white ink
its vowels of erasure,
red finches scatter seed
the memory of desire.

Along with *aah* and *ooh*
consonants are underground
alphabet of weather
palms a heart in its hand.

2.

G–d is your shadow.
You move—G–d moves
sweeping the floor
paring apples
spooning the honey.

3.

Large house at dusk, bare trees.
You're bleeding from the gut.
I can't make sense of human life
a crimson brocade in the fading light.

4.

G-d wakes up
like a drunk
shouting.

The alphabet is ziggurat
pale blue as dusk.

Violet on the spectrum
curved heart, aleph climbs

through the air
in the hours
before Babel.

※

Writing on Salt

oddly purposive arrangement of stones water
    left behind

mirage can be mathematically predicted

who placed these beer bottles like Stonehenge?

I filled a baggie with sand

day after day the wind visited me like a busybody

an insufficiency of tears

the invisible left a glyph

time might not be moving the distance was so vast

the poem seemed like something that was outside
    of me

an alphabet has no numeric value

blue was an inadequate word in this field of vision

metal outline of a man, target shot full of holes

the army built a city of sand and bombed it

I couldn't have believed this emptiness if I hadn't
    slept without dreams

mist rose from what once was sea as if it still was

※

In Translation

Eclipse of the moon by the earth tonight,
buckles lost from both my shoes,
I mark the book with a postcard of the Pleiades,
who has erased the stanzas from this page?

※

Supernova

in the Crab Nebula
over Chaco Canyon.

This new star
appears not only in the sky
But marked in stone.

Why do these roads
appear to lead nowhere?

Venus rising
between two monoliths
right before our eyes.

※

Jacob Wrestles the Angel

Not just a man with two wives
not just a twin plagued by doubles
Jacob becomes a leaflet
in the street, tulips
sent to a sick friend,
the odd kindness
with which my neighbor
greets me, telling me
there are too many apricots on her tree
would I take some.

Jacob becomes flesh again,
now it's your turn
to stay up all night
and your turn to limp
all morning.

※

Vision at the Shaffer Hotel

A starlit neon sign
dusk lights the words
that light the line.

No monk's cell
just a room
in an old hotel.

Still in my mind's eye
I see Chinese brushstroke cliffs
a waterfall

and see
what solitude
sees in me.

※

Vegas

These mute guardians
of the self—
headless generalissimo
decapitated colonial statue,
or a wall niched
with breasts, torso
like a psycho killer's antiquities.

Real bamboo
fake bamboo
real noodles
real waitress
whose real mother
has hysterical blindness
from her place in history.

Fountain of Buddhas
illuminated cones

a real job for a woman:
dealing baccarat
driving a cab
dancing on a pole.

A water buffalo
designed of topiary flowers
a ten foot statue

of one of the happy Immortals
pagoda, golden koi
a real barrier gate.

Yellow-tailed skeleton of a fish
(think neon)
homeless man begging with a cardboard sign VET
the fountains at the Bellagio
dancing to Copeland swell of notes—
"'tis a gift to be simple"
an irony lost in the spray
JESUS! JESUS! JESUS!
the street corner preachers exhort us
as Venus rises in the east
(as does everything)
over Caesar's.

Dozens of brides
short, young, old, plump
bosomy, smiling, drunk
with groomsmen in kilts or tuxes
and just one feckless tattooed groom
to hold on to.
It is Valentine's Day after all
(and you are
in bed with me)

my dream
that you can't use a capital I
anymore in a poem
because there is no self.

Now you are so deep in America
you cannot get out

it's raining
and I pick up
a spray of purple velvet orchids
in the street

※

At the Next Table

Girl in the yellow dress at the Caffe Tazza
says that tantric sex has knocked her silly;
her boyfriend looks so ordinary
drinking foam off caffè latte.

※

Acoma

You've gone to Acoma
high mesa, grit in the eye
wind in the alley of dust
city of potters against the sky
where stars leak through the paneless windows.
Pericardium surrounds the heart;
you my deer carcass, my bison corpse
still warm, that I crawl into
against the wind and snow, the tundra, night.
You, my house of thigh bones
my slim knife
my pair of quartz stones, fire flint.
What I mean to say is:
I love you that much.
What I mean to say is:
I love you.

※

Valentine for My Daughter

I did not know that I could love like this
love like a juggernaut upon an iron track
before you came my heart stayed in my body
did not grow legs to walk the world without me.

※

Writing on Stone

The circle with dots
scratched in desert varnish
might be narrative
or instruction fallen
from the Pleiades.

Stars crack pinpoints
in the shell of night,
a daytime moon
hangs over the lava crystals,
cracked pressure ridge,
meadowlark, lizard, sotol.

The artist who can no longer see
but whose hand can move
guides someone else's
in the blue red or green.

These shapes
are not telling a story
but rather
seem to sing—niggun—
a melody without words.

※

Three Rivers

Lightning
carves a petroglyph
in the cloud

the fighter jet
rises behind the ridge
of imagined stone

carved dancer's mask
katsina
pales under the sheen

of rainwater
which for a moment
erases

all trace
of us.

※

Lightning Field Haiku

Thirty-three years
beneath these poles—
how many rabbit holes?

horizon clearing—
it must have been you I saw
out in the field

telephone poles
highway
the flash-by dreams

was that piece of bone
always here
by the door jamb?

the same light
comes through the chinks
of the cabin

awaiting departure
as if that were
news of the world

even the word
vastness
underestimates

I saw your hat
walk away
turn back

※

At the Observatory

Three little girls
ran up the hill
as Venus was setting
as if for a better view.
Through the telescope I saw
the planet as a crescent
twinkling in the atmosphere.
Pointing at the center
of the Milky Way
saw stars born and tied together
like siblings or aspen trees
Twin stars—one yellow,
one blue of Albireo
(eye of Cygnus the Swan)
clear sight of Jupiter
with its four moons
that let Galileo understand
we are not the center of the universe.

A fair-haired girl
was reading a book
by the light of the setting evening star
and later by her cell phone.
"You'll ruin your eyes!"
I exclaimed as if I were her mother.
She laughed and turned the page.

※

Rooftop

Dusky moth, brown velveteen
wings marked with a face
to scare a predator
clinging to the red stucco wall
of the roof patio, where I smoke
a rare cigarette

African thorn tree
in a pot
trunk encrusted
with dozens of sharp
tiny breasts that bite
in armoring....

The way we can surprise ourselves.

※

Border Crossing

River shifts and floods,
the little mission church
on the Mexican side
now finds itself in Texas—silver foil onion dome,
colorful corn and stepped clouds
painted on the plaster walls,
a fat white candle for the Virgin.

The border crosses us—our faith, our expectations
as Milky Way spills
across the winter sky
the starry footprint of an antelope
inspires the throw
of an atlatl.
Arcturus herding far-off twinkle
Cassiopeia's zigzag above ocotillo dagger leaves
on solstice
old boomerang of stars.

※

Bread Mystery

In the uncountable alphabet
bitter pine forest of words
sans serif
without butter or jam

one day we'll eat earth
and cry for more!
drink tea through a sugar cube
in italics

how is the strand of wheat
bent heavy with seed
supposed to speak
without being ground?

The night was aphasic
and the day
also said nothing
had nothing to say.

It's winter, and the wild
girl goddess has gone underground.
"Why me" is not a question
that bears repeating.

This dough will rise
in the starter of spring
and its crust can be opened
by the mouse teeth of desire

white bread like the moon
in the eastern sky
full, sliced, gone—
round again.

※

Dark Star Park

after Nancy Holt

We walk through granite spheres
some things have happened
some things have not.

You, me, your widowed father
it's humid
in suburban Rosslyn, Virginia.

Each year I pass
the anniversary of my death
not knowing, yet, to light a candle

office building windows reflect the light
time is no palindrome
can't be read equally backwards and forwards.

These globes won't roll
suddenly across the watered grass
and into traffic

much as I might wish
for satori
or at least excitement.

※

Even After He Went Blind

Degas bought Rembrandt etchings
kept them crated and stored
against one wall of the studio.

Sometime I think
I'll awake once and for all
to this world.

※

Scenes

motel night
in the paper cup, an inch
of sumi ink

moonless
until the clouds
part

she said: prop a chair
under the doorknob to keep out
all that vastness

untrained
hand and eye
I draw the mountains

my father tells me
he can no longer remember
last night's dream

out of range
of the familiar oldies
station

※

Color Field (neon, Dan Flavin)

I'll bow to you
from the edge of blue.

These bars which separate us
might just be colored light (pink and green).

In the last piece
turquoise dominates

purple triangles push off
the edge of the screen.

Who knew it would be so difficult
and this easy?

※

Brattle Street Theater

When the woman at the dinner party
took out her eyeballs
and put them in the wineglass—
that's when I wished
I hadn't come to the Brattle alone
for the matinee
of Bergman's *Hour of the Wolf.*
The Brattle was run down
red velvet chairs with seats stuck up
and derelicts
paid three bucks for a snooze
off the Cambridge streets.

Here, I whiled away my youth
not reading *La Chartreuse de Parme*
in French or studying
the classification of shellfish
but rather at the double feature movies
seeing all the black and white
Bergman ever made.

And then stepping out
onto the street
upper Brattle just a few blocks from my dorm
bare trees in winter, leafy in spring
the door swung from illuminated figured darkness
into east coast light late afternoon.

Years later, this scene
answered the riddle:
what is the self?
Answered my koan.

※

Forest Fire Sijo

Forest fire smoke obscures the mountains, we wait for rain.
All day the car radio plays only "Riders on the Storm."
From four hundred miles west wind carries the ash
    of love letters.

※

Saranac Lake

We sleep in the cool room
off a corridor, in a former
TB sanitarium
turned hotel
with a wide
wraparound porch
for wrapped patients
and a quality
of whiteness.

On the way to the bathroom
a statue of Cupid and Psyche
neoclassical replica
locked in a wild embrace
and although you don't
wear wings
pinned to your skinny shoulders
I did know you well
when you were a boy
and I was mortal.

Red turret of a house
reflected in the lake,
a miniature
Adirondack chair
waiting for a child
to settle in it,
a child called happiness.

※

Genius Loci: Salem, NY

This is ordinary life
certainly not
at its worst:
hardware store with bins of nails, tiger lilies wild
by the embankment
train tracks, but possibly
no train and when I close my eyes
and nap before the afternoon thunderstorm
I might not be anywhere at all
but rather in one of many spots
I've been before.

Aristotle thought place gave order to the world—
at the cafe, behind me
conversation is slow moving, focused on
"now, when *did* your folks buy that land,
'38? '41?," and this the last century.
I turn and look into the woman's withered
    cheerful face
as she says: "Well, like my sister I have the arthritis
she's ninety-three, I'm ninety-two,"
and smiles above her coffee cup.

Utopia may mean "no place"
but that's certainly not
how they feel about it
up by the Vermont border.
I thought there was a map.
There is no map
although you want me still, I still want you,
and each line waiting for its rhyme
it is not space
that pulls me down but time.

※

Black Tideline

lace spread
mantilla on the endless
white sand

sandpipers
tiny angel wing shells
size of my pinkie
fingernail

oil spill
faraway, and
near
washes up

as will
everything
eventually.

※

Santa Rosa Island

Beach town off season
Christmas day rain
white sand, palm, the Gulf of Mexico

humped pelican shapes, long causeway, barrier island
we sit in the car in the parking lot
blasting Ode to Joy.

※

Swan Lake/Bonneville

Wild black ducks
sleep on their own reflections
floating on the flooded salt flats

the same in the city duck pond
with gleaming mallards
white geese

and an intrusion of a line
of black-necked Canada geese
dropping from a V in the sky

the prima ballerina
photographed as dawn
fills the Great Basin

stiff tutu and unbound hair
arms twisted up
she dances Swan Lake.

✳

Writing Workshop

Buson's haiku
about the javelin holders
in the cold—

all the veterans
in the class
perk up

even though
right here
it is spring.

※

Monument

Long park, territory
of taggers, and the mute
passers-by who
without spray cans
leave no mark

not just place but
narrative
someone died, the kids say
writing not on air but on
electrical exchange station

something went wrong

a formal
designated history
on plaques includes
one for pioneer Jews,
it doesn't say
they fled failed revolutions
free-thinkers, built no mikvahs
just burial plots from the Woodsmen of the World

now defaced
with white paint:
JEW

this place, if you look beneath,
simply a station
from which you depart
perhaps arrive.

※

Neglected airport motel

mild Thanksgiving Day

television
blares
the president

little volcanoes
out to the west
of Albuquerque

in the Bible drawer
also
a Bhagavad Gita

at breakfast
just me and
some Navajo ladies
heading
    elsewhere.

※

Visitor

On the east side of the highway
a woman parks by the descansos
takes out her Taos hand drum
and in her fringed jacket
begins beating a rhythm
for the dead.

I, who am driving north,
burst into tears
wondering if this
is an anniversary.
I see those memorials
every day
but never before
someone who has come
to greet the sprits.

Across Abiquiú dam
beneath the cosmic shape
known as Pedernal
all I can call up
is my fear and
my love of wandering.

Not a tent, not a yurt, not a tipi
my body
isn't exactly a square or a triangle
rather a body-shaped hole
I sometimes fall through.

Tidying up
I find neatly zipped
into a pocket of my backpack
boarding passes
from a flight
I don't remember
ever taking.

※

Signal Fire

A plume of smoke
in the mountain
behind town—
I'd just stepped out
of the movie
13 Assassins and
enjoyed samurai
hacking each other
and wondered
about my own death
on a summer's afternoon
feeling content
until driving home
I saw it to the north
conflagration
and knew exactly
where it was
what canyon
like seeing a look of terrible pain
cross the face of
someone you love.

Each direction
should have its colors
and signs
but here
everything cardinal
is fire
red phoenix of summer solstice
wildfire
with its message
    hexagram
drawn with a stick in dirt
(your fortune is crossed).
The palm reader
or Sister Rosa
just around the corner off Sierra Vista
sees a small bonfire
burn the hearts off the cards.

Or…
a column of smoke by day
of flame
by night
which leads across a barren wasteland
but—to where?
charred needles
dropped from a great height
by the prevailing winds.

A physicist
a child on a swing
try googling
"pictures of cities"
find Nineveh (where God's hand was stayed)
Nagasaki
where it was not
try googling
"on what day will I die?"
or "G-d sends rain"
try prayer
or just sleeping through it…
I pack my passport
three pairs of underpants
and not much else
won't save the photograph
from its edge
curling in flame.

Lodgepole pine sealed with resin
ponderosa forest
was savannah
before the grazing cattle
a crown fire
burns ghosts of aspen
those silvery trees
that must char
before they sprout.

Earth's divination
reveals destruction
more than a change
a renewal
wind in black fire
on white fire
day, night
a compass needle spins
without foresight.

※

The Chinese Garden

Chinatown seems gone,
boarded up, destroyed, abandoned:
homeless tents, the stink
of piss. And apparently
a willingness to let people
live like garbage
among prosperity.

A rusted bridge
spans the river
but will collapse
next time the earth shakes
from its hot core. This place
lacks local gods
has no knowledge
of who or what
to placate.

Half-moon arch, dark rattling
lotus pods, red fruit
of the mountain camellia
yellow leaves that
float on air and
golden carp
that leap

from muck
like the lily pads
from muddy water
something good can come
out of the heart—
but is that a statement
or a question?
Serendipity or art?

I've paid admission, that's for sure
and in this life
I'll also expect
an exit visa won't come cheap.
But still, we're here
besides *Tai Hu* rocks
limestone mined from a fresh-water lake
whose holes allow life force
to freely flow
like the leak windows
from one courtyard to the next.

The stone bench is
too damp and narrow
to sit on long,
conversation
interrupted by old age's need
to stretch.
And since it's time for lunch
walk out into the street
unable to pretend
that this is anything
but empire's end.

※

3 Sijo

When will I see you again? In a dream? In the face of a child?
Crossing the red bridge, talk of spirits brings tears to our eyes,
autumn forgives summer for leaving the far blue foothills.

The small pine, late pink roses with uncurled petals,
far view of mountains, cloudless sky an effortless blue,
the best way to be my friend is to want to talk about death.

You want to see the solar eclipse with me, your oldest friend,
we'll go to San Ysidro, the slot canyon's darkness and light
we've grown so old this might be the last time we meet to say
    good-bye.

※

All it takes is rain

to turn these southern Colorado mountains
into a Song dynasty
painting

you watch a bear
amble away down an alley
and have to restrain yourself
from following

later, looking for Mercury
you count the stars
to make sure
the Shabbat you don't keep
is over.

※

Devils Tower

Creation remains a mystery to me.
I saw my godson born one night in early spring
out from between his mother's legs
looked into his newborn eyes
and wondered: where did you come from?
Across ten centimeters of dilating flesh?
Across the eons of a cervix?

Was I in search of healing
at Devils Tower, Wyoming
as if this was Lourdes?
I took my cane, my crippled self,
my shrinking life expectancy
and for a few minutes believed I was whole
and could circumambulate
this whole huge stupa of volcanic rock.

When I was a child, I saw it in a book
one of those Time Life
series on the natural world
a volume that arrived by mail each month.
There it was, starkly rising,
my mother described it, half-accurately
as the core of a volcano
something we certainly lacked
in Bergen County, New Jersey.
But we didn't lack desire
like the two climbers

halfway up that monolith
roped in in the photograph.
What made it? Even the geologists
do not agree.
Some call it laccolith
that mushroom cloud of igneous rock
that swells but cannot
reach the surface.
The lines of hexagons
volcanic crystal
appear as scratch marks
of a gigantic bear.

Prayers hang in fabric knots
from birch, burned branches
like Jerusalem's kotel
the only standing wall of the temple
where every crevice is stuffed
full of prayers on paper.
An old man with a broom comes
and sweeps them away at night—
he is ancient
lives alone in a little apartment.
Can this sweeper still be alive?
Maybe he is immortal.

At dusk dozens of vultures
roost in pine trees
their iconic humped shape
as characteristic as this Bear Lodge tower
turning pinker at sunset
in fields of yellow flowers
that suddenly smell
both sweeter and more sharply.

Vultures circle and float
along updrafts.
The day is hot, and fine.
These scavengers may not be
heroic as hawks
but are divine.

※

Rust Never Sleeps

I lie in the expensive bed
in the airport motel, serene
in hypnogogic state. In the middle of the night
awake, feeling trouble
multiply within my cells
in the body's tender parts. I dream
a friend of mine, a mediator,
is trying to mitigate a quarrel
between a man and a woman. Numerous
people live within me, along with disease
and even health. I see you in the early morning light
carting your entire personality
through security, and on to
elsewhere.

※

While You Were Out

Naked woman with an owl on her head
The angel left the sick girl
Facades contained both numbers and alphabets
An Islamic silver ring inscribed "thanks to G-d"
A window on something else
Bands of color
No allegory
Vertical landscape (erosion and continental drift)
The gravel had my gratitude
At the end of the ladder butterflies
Obscured the Chinese characters
You couldn't locate your history on the tree ring
But took a Greyhound bus away from solitude

※

Score for the Audience

I'd like to compose a piece of music
for the audience:

a cough, three in a row,
the noise of small random objects
dropping out of a purse or pocket
sighs
and unsilenced cell phones
going off in patterned ringtones—
a bird call, the opening notes of a
golden oldie,
chimes, church bells.

Add in construction from the street,
the gas company
retrofitting lines
as noisy as if the road crew
were attempting to excavate Atlantis or
Mycenae but in the wrong location.

Now, a car alarm. It stops.
It starts again.

Sounds get wilder and wilder.
The audience applauds
between movements, between notes
while on stage the orchestra
murmurs "bravo!"
in its sleep.

※

The Pleasure of Travel

Reading *Gawain and the Green Knight*
in a restaurant
called Little Cambodia
in Salida, Colorado
and eating a bowl
of Vietnamese pho
noticing
the overflow tables
next door
in a vast space
which houses, for some
unknown reason,
two shrouded
full-size
pool tables.

※

A Final Task

Follow the rules of the underworld:

don't eat or drink

don't stop
to help the old man
gathering wood
who has your father's face

don't try to save
the desperate swimmer
in the river Lethe
even if you went to high school together.

A silver egg
in a pile of ash
might be called
"Phoenix"
or "Forest Fire"

the way a lost
earring
might imply
a much larger
disaster.

It is dangerous
to mark off
Xs on the calendar
lines on the prison wall
and by this invite
"before" and "after."

Each day
find another
mourning dove feather
in the yard
and add it
to a piece about time.

※

Via Menemsha

Red sail,
dark, actual
in the twilit channel
ebbing still

blood burnt west
full moon harvest
the trawlers, water-torn,
returning home.

My heart, white stone:
asleep,
cycladic, eyeless
sculpted to itself

dirt road of moonlight
trees in darkness
no stopping, no path
sea's body, pathless.

※

Ring of Fire

We went up to San Ysidro campground
to see the annular eclipse.
The gate was unlocked,
kids were running about, with dogs,
I drank a cup of hot tea
from my son-in-law
in the RV. We had NASA-approved
glasses, and welding goggles,
and sat in our lawn chairs
all pointing in the same direction
like the heads on Easter Island.

My four-year-old granddaughter
yelled "It's starting"
and had a longer
attention span
than I'd predicted. After all
at some point, everyone turned away
and you told me to look behind us
to see Venus shining
as the sky darkened.

And then some of the kids
who'd been watching the eclipse projection
got bored
and one boy put the cardboard box
over his head
and biked around blind
except for the tiny pinhole
through which we'd expected to see
the universe.

※

Midnight. Pee in a can.

Outside in the dark
all the Sangre de Cristos
white-capped.

※

Just Jump

To leap from the lip of the granite quarry
is to show-off, become a corpse, touch the angel
of burning air on the way down.
Pick one.

To break the surface of the water
is to acquire a body
to brush domes and towers with bare feet
to change your name to "Return To Center."

All of the above.

※

I selected these poems from those that were never collected into a book or chapbook. Some of these poems first appeared in the following magazines:

> "Fever Tropics" in *Blackberry*
> "Darkness Darkness" in *Crowdancing*, and set to
> 　　music on the *Poetry Devils* cassette
> "Not Watching the Eclipse" in *Christian Science
> 　　Monitor*
> "the brass Tara" in *Windchimes*
> "Acoma" in *Nexus*, *Poetry Devils* cassette, *6 Poets
> 　　Reading* from Fish Drum
> "Valentine for My Daughter" in *Ant Farm*
> "blue numbers" in *Hodge Lodge*
> "White Psalm" in *House Organ*
> "Jacob Wrestles the Angel" in *Mimakim*
> "Vegas" in *Dorado*
> "Tent Rocks" in *Modern Literature* (India)
> "Black Tideline" in *The Rag*
> "Signal Fire" in *Chokecherries*
> "Swan Lake/Bonneville" in *Bohemia*
> "Scenes" (partial) in *Heron's Nest*
> "Bread Mystery" installed as text and audio by
> 　　Axle Contemporary in Site Santa Fe

Some of these poems were written at Yaddo; CLUI (Center for Land Use Interpretation) in Wendover, Utah; Colorado Art Ranch (Salida residency); Lannan Foundation residency in Marfa, Texas; Salem Arts Works (New York); National Parks artist-in-residency program in the Everglades, Florida; and as part of the Road Trips to the Moon project with Teresa Neptune, Neptune Gallery, Canyon Road, Santa Fe, New Mexico.

※

Miriam Sagan is the author of more than thirty books of poetry, fiction, and memoir. She is a two-time winner of the New Mexico/Arizona Book Award as well as a recipient of the City of Santa Fe Mayor's Award for Excellence in the Arts and a New Mexico Literary Arts Gratitude Award. She has been a writer-in-residence at four U.S. national parks, Yaddo, MacDowell, Kura Studio in Japan, Gullkistan in Iceland, and a dozen other remote and interesting places.

She works with text and sculptural installation as part of the mother/daughter creative team Maternal Mitochondria (with Isabel Winson-Sagan) in venues ranging from RV parks to galleries. She founded the creative writing program at Santa Fe Community College and directed it until her retirement. Her poetry has been set to music for the Santa Fe Women's Chorus, incised on stoneware for two haiku pathways, and projected as video inside an abandoned building during the pandemic under the auspices of Vital Spaces.

※

Casa Urraca Press publishes poetry, fiction, creative nonfiction, and other works by authors we believe in. New Mexico and the U.S. Southwest are rich in creative and literary talent, and the rest of the world deserves to experience our perspectives. So we champion books that belong in the conversation—books with the power, compassion, and variety to bring very different people closer together.

We are proudly centered in the high desert somewhere near Abiquiú, New Mexico. Visit us online to read more from our authors, browse all editions of our books, and register for writing workshops at casaurracapress.com.

※